D0871910

JUL   2015

Drawing Is Awesome!

DRAWING AWESOME
CARTOON
CHARACTERS

Damien Toll

WINDMILL
BOOKS

Contents

Introduction

Drawing is a fun and rewarding hobby for both children and adults alike. This book is designed to show how easy it is to draw great pictures by building them in simple stages.

What you will need

Only basic materials are required for effective drawing. These are:

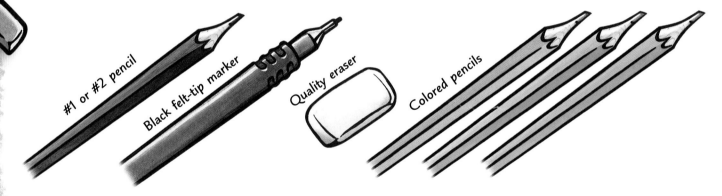

#1 or #2 pencil   Black felt-tip marker   Quality eraser   Colored pencils

These will be enough to get started. Avoid buying the cheapest pencils. Their leads often break off in the sharpener, even before they can be used. The leads are also generally too hard, making them difficult to see on the page.

Cheap erasers also cause problems by smudging rather than erasing. This often leaves a permanent stain on the paper. By spending a little more on art supplies in these areas, problems such as these can be avoided.

When purchasing a black marker, choose one to suit the size of your drawings. If you draw on a large scale, a thick felt-tip marker may be necessary. If you draw on a medium scale, a medium-point marker will do and if on a small scale, a 0.3 mm, 0.5 mm, 0.7 mm, or 0.8 mm felt-tip marker will work best.

The Stages

Simply follow the lines drawn in orange on each stage using your #1 or #2 pencil. The blue lines on each stage show what has already been drawn in the previous stages.

1.

2.

3.

In the final stage the drawing has been outlined in black and the simple shape and wire-frame lines erased. The shapes are only there to help us build the picture. We finish the picture by drawing over the parts we need to make it look like our subject with the black marker, and then erasing all the simple shape lines.

Included here is a sketch of a running boy as it would be originally drawn by an artist.

These are how all the characters in this book were originally worked out and drawn. The orange and blue stages you see above are just a simplified version of this process. The drawing here has been made by many quick pencil strokes working over each other to make the line curve smoothly. It does not matter how messy it is as long as the artist knows the general direction of the line to follow with the black marker at the end. The pencil lines are erased and a clean outline is left. Therefore, do not be afraid to make a little mess with your #1 or #2 pencil, as long as you do not press so hard that you cannot erase it afterwards.

4.

5.

Grids made of squares are set behind each stage in this book. Make sure to draw a grid lightly on your page so it does not press into the paper and show up after being erased. Artist tips have also been added to show you some simple things that can make your drawing look great. Have fun!

Thinker

Thinkers come up with ways to improve the way we live. He usually has a furrowed brow emphasizing his deep thoughts and his revolutionary ideas. Or, he may just be thinking about what to have for lunch.

1.

Begin by drawing a grid with two equal squares going across and four down.

Draw in the shape for the head with his ear. Notice his brow line is close to the top of his head. Add his upturned mouth. Draw in his jacket.

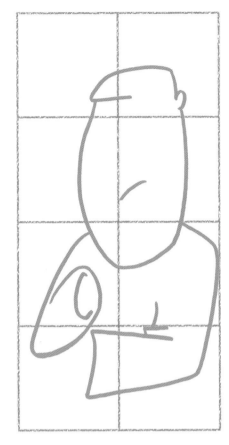

2.

Add some hair and his sideburns. Draw some creases in his brow. Add his nose and eyes. Draw in his hands and shirt cuff to complete this stage.

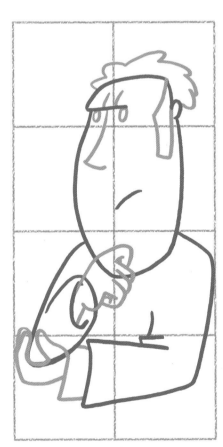

3.

Draw a line for his jacket cuff on his right hand. Add his glasses and a line for the inside of his ear to finish.

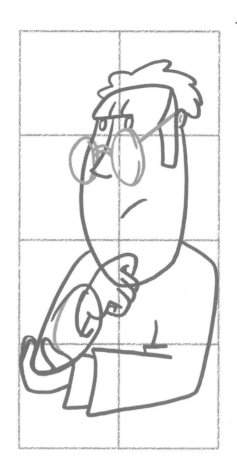

4.

Thinkers aren't known for their excitement, so they wear conservative colors like whites, grays, and blacks.

Sporty Grandma

Grannies are often thought to be fragile and content, relaxing in a rocking chair. Cartooning allows us the freedom to go outside the normal boundaries of reality and make characters do things they never would do. So what better way to do this than to have granny busting out on a fast break in a basketball game?

1.

Begin by drawing a grid with three equal squares going across and down.

Draw in the eyes and the eyebrows. Add the small nose and ear.

Draw in the cheeks and chin.

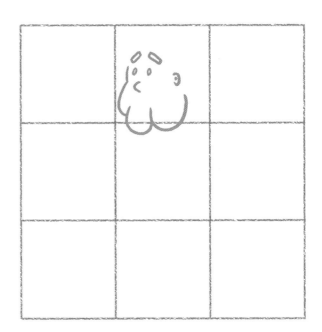

2.

Add the hair and mouth. Draw the frills around her neck and the arms.

Draw the frills at the end of her arms, and cone shapes going down to her hands. Notice how simple the hands are. Draw them in.

Complete the rest of this stage by drawing clothes and buttons.

3.

Draw in the basketball and put a rounded cross on it.

Add the dress and the thin legs coming out from it. Check to see if your drawing is correct and move on to the next stage.

4.

Draw in the round lines on the ball. Add her glasses and her handbag. Draw the shoes and the dust-puff lines to show that she's moving quickly. Add the rounded movement lines to finish the stage.

5.

Grannies usually have gray or white hair. They do not usually wear bright energetic colors, but since this is a cartoon, you could make her any color you like. Happy coloring!

Pirate

Pirates are mean seafarers who are well known for their rough looks and attitudes. Wooden legs, hooks for hands, and eye patches are commonly associated with pirates.

1.

Begin by drawing a grid with three equal squares going across and down.

Draw in the eye and eyebrow followed by the nose. Draw in the other eye patch. Draw the ear and the large beard around to his eye patch.

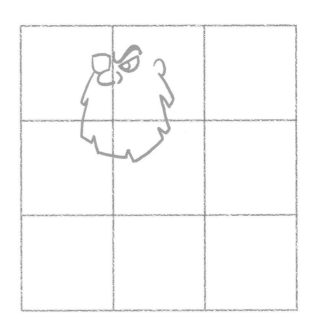

2.

Draw in the mouth and the head scarf: add the jacket top and the arms. Study the hands so you can draw them correctly.

3.

Draw in the sword and sheath.

Add the rest of the jacket. Draw in the trousers. Add the shape for the top of the boot.

4.

Black out some teeth and add his wooden leg. Draw in the rest of his boot to finish this stage.

5.

You could have this pirate standing on the deck of his ship, ready for a sword fight.

Wacky Wombat

Wacky characters are very popular in animation. The character doesn't need to closely resemble the real animal, just as long as it has the animal's basic features. These simple colored characters are commonly used in animated cartoons.

1.

Begin by drawing a grid with three equal squares going across and down.

Draw three shapes: a large circle, a small circle and a roundish square. Check that they are in the correct position on the grid.

2.

Draw his eye pupils and a circle to define the highlights in his eyes. Add his head shape and ear, and continue the line under his nose and his mouth.

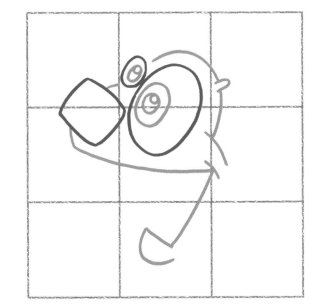

3.

Draw in the eyebrows far above his eyes and other ear. Draw the teeth and a line for the inner mouth. Add his body shape down to his little legs and pointy toes.

4.

Draw in a rectangle shape for the highlight on his nose. Add some droplets of water near his mouth. Draw the other arm and the noisemaker in the wombat's hand.

5.

Wombats are a darker brown than this. The realistic dark brown color would make this wombat look heavy. Since we don't want him heavy, but looking energetic, we've made him a lighter color brown.

Cute Girl

Innocence and simplicity is often associated with cuteness. A happy-go-lucky personality and a love of life go hand in hand with this type of character. Shrugged shoulders and slightly pointed-in feet emphasize this attitude.

1.

Begin by drawing a grid with two equal squares going across and four down.

Draw in the eyes first and then the small eyebrows. Add the shape of the cheeks and face. Draw in the hairline. Draw the neck and finish this stage with the little nose.

2.

Add in the top of the hair and the mouth. Draw the hand on the mouth and then the arm.

Draw the t-shirt and curved lines for the hips and legs.

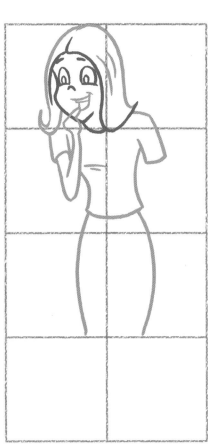

3.

Draw in the arm and hand. Study the hand here to see how simple it is.

Add the rest of the skirt and the legs and feet.

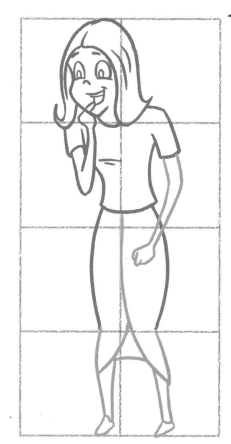

4.

When outlining your drawing, be careful to only ink the lines you need. Color to your heart's content. You may even want to put a different pattern on the skirt.

Mad Scientist

Working deep in his secret laboratory, this chemical cocktail-making madman is growing more insane with each devious thought. He is obsessed with his plan to take over the world. Wild hair and a torn lab coat are the result of past experiments gone wrong. Could this be the moment before this mad scientist's next unfortunate event?

1.

Begin by drawing a grid with three equal squares going across and down.

Start this stage by drawing the closed eye's eyebrow. Draw in the line for the closed eye and surrounding cheek and brow. Draw in the other eye and add the nose. Draw in the ear and mouth. Check that everything looks correct before moving on to the next stage.

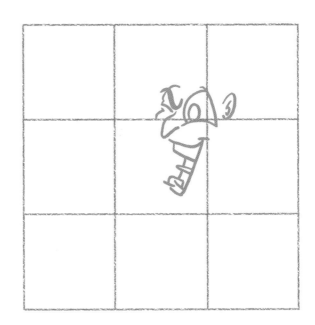

2.

Draw in the beard and bottom part of the open eye. Add the eyelid above the eye. Draw some crazy hair all around from his brow to his beard. Finish this stage by drawing in the curved arm.

3.

Draw the hand and test tube. Add the collar of his lab coat and the flared-out bottom of it on either side. Draw in his legs and tiny feet.

4.

Draw in the other test tube and hand. Draw in his torn coat arm right up to his brow. Add the steam to finish this stage.

5.

Could the green on this scientist be a reflection of the nuclear ooze glowing from the countertop he is standing in front of? Or maybe some sort of radiation machine he has invented?

Running Boy

Kids love to play, which includes running as fast as they can. Running for the fun of it is a simple pleasure for these overly energetic children. This boy could be racing other kids, chasing a ball, or trying to escape from an imaginative monster in hot pursuit!

1.

Begin by drawing a grid with three equal squares going across and down.

Draw in the shape of the head with the hair. Add the sleeves of his shirt on a slight angle.

2.

Draw in his arms and hands. Notice there isn't much detail on his clenched fist.

Draw in his shorts, leg, and shoe.

3.

Draw in his eyes, nose and mouth. Put in a squiggly line for the inside of his ear. Add the other leg. Draw in the closer leg sock line to finish.

Artist Tip:

Cartoons have a lot of gaps around them. These gaps highlight action and movement. Notice this boy's legs are in an extreme pose: both are off the ground in full stride. The action is shown by the gap between the boy and the ground, where there is a shadow underneath. This enhances the feel of movement and speed. Have a look at some comic strips and you're sure to find this principle.

4.

Kids are often associated with primary colors. These are blue, red, and yellow. These colors are bold, bright and energetic. They also work very well together.

Sheriff

"This 'ere town ain't big enuff for the tew of us, so one of us 'as gotta go!" This sheriff is pumped in a ready stance to take on the outlaws in a quick-draw duel. He relies on his fast reflexes and sharpshooting to maintain justice in the West. Are you ready to draw?

1.

Begin by drawing a grid with four equal squares going across and three down.

Start with a rounded triangle for his hat. Draw the arms in a wide curving arc, starting close to the top of his hat brim. When drawing the arms, make them wider at the top and gradually thinner when they reach the wrist. Draw in his torso and the shape for his face.

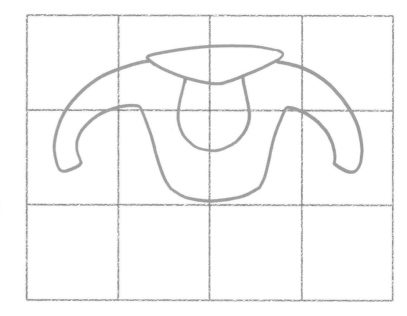

2.

Draw in the crown of his hat and his vest. Add the sleeves bunching up at his wrists. Draw in his belt and trousers.

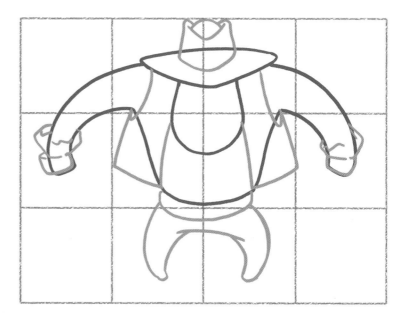

3.

Draw in two half circles under his hat for his eyes. Put in his nose and pushed-up lip. Draw two circles for his badge. Add his gun holsters at his side and the bullets around his belt. Put in his shirt buttons. Draw his ready hands and finish this stage with his feet.

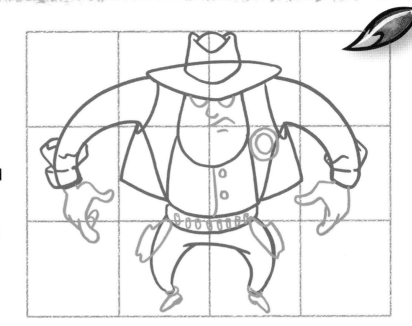

4.

Add the guns in his holsters, with some movement lines around them and his fingers. Draw in the star on his badge. Add some whiskers around his chin and some dots for whiskers on his face. Draw the pupils in his eyes to finish.

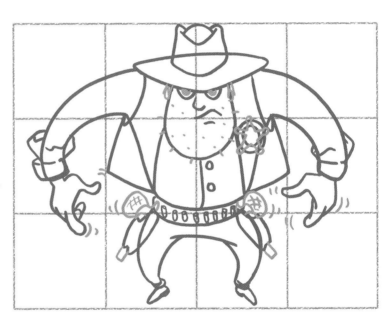

5.

Cowboys wear leather belts, jackets and shoes. These are often tan (light brown) or black. They also often wear blue jeans. The "bad guys" in films often wear black.

Baby

Babies have very distinct features, which makes them great for cartooning. They have huge heads and large eyes. They are very chubby and can often be seen crawling around wearing only a white diaper and sporting a giant safety pin. Their only accessory is a pacifier, which is most likely found on the ground beside their stroller.

1.

Begin by drawing a grid with three equal squares going across and down.

Draw in a three-quarter circle for the head. Add two shapes for the ears. Draw in the stretched oval shape for the chin.

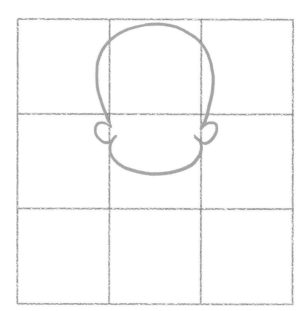

2.

Draw in the big eyes and the eyebrows. Add the little nose and the inside of the ear lines.

Draw the shapes for the feet.

3.

Add the lines on the feet. Draw in the chubby legs and the oval shape for the diaper. Draw two lines up from the diaper for the baby's chest.

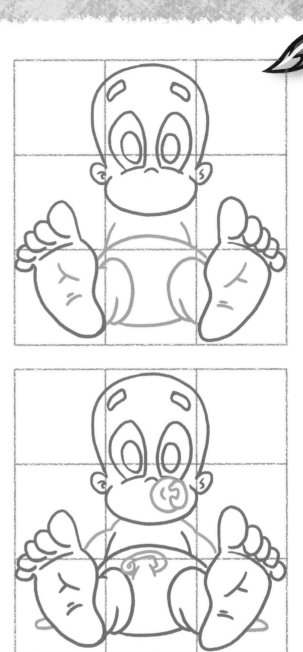

4.

Draw the shoulders and arms and the bits near the feet. These are the baby's hands.

Draw in the pacifier to the right of his face.

Add the safety pin and you're ready to ink!

5.

Babies have blue eyes when they are born. They also wear white diapers. If you look closely, you will notice that the diaper is not perfectly white. By coloring it very lightly with gray or blue, it can still seem white, but more realistic.

Villain

Evilly inclined, these villains are devious figures. They devise ways to subdue mankind so they can control the world. Their ideas never seem to go as planned because of the hero, who always seems to be present just before the moment the villain will reach glory.

1.

Begin by drawing a grid with two equal squares going across and four down.

Start with the villain's eyes, eyebrows and nose. Add his large rounded brow. Draw in his mouth and ear.

2.

Draw his beard and the top of his head. Add in his huge collar, pointing into a "V" at his chest. Draw his shoulders and his curved arm sleeves. Add thin wrists and a ball for his hands.

3.

Draw in some squiggly lines for his fingers. Finish off by adding his coat. Notice how it is draped along the floor.

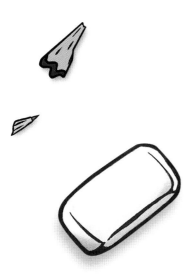

4.

Villains usually wear fancy darker colored clothes. They rarely wear bright colors. This helps them seem more sinister.

Henchman

These goons are a villain's number-one recruits. They are generally big, strong, and unable to think for themselves, which makes them perfect to carry out the villain's every command. Henchmen are also bodyguards for the villain and are always dressed in black suits.

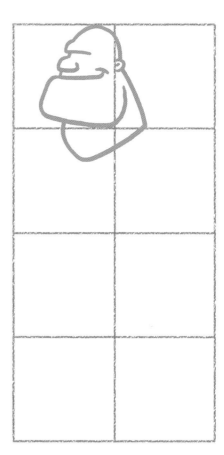

1.

Begin by drawing a grid with two equal squares going across and four down.

Draw in the face, making the chin big and the rest of the head small. Draw in little ears and a thick neck.

2.

Draw in his collar and shoulders. Add his left arm and then continue with his chest, stomach, and other arm.

3.

Draw in his hand. Draw the trousers getting smaller as they go down and add tiny feet.

4.

Outline and color in your henchman as you like. Here we have used a near-black on the suit that fades into blue, and then white on the highlights.

King

These rulers of the medieval world have many personalities. There was nothing more appreciated by the people than a jolly king. They dressed in large, heavy robes and often wore heavy jewelry such as rings on their fingers. They also carry a large golden rod called a scepter.

1.

Begin by drawing a grid with three equal squares going across and down.

Draw in the eyes followed by the nose and the mouth. Add the eyebrows to finish this stage.

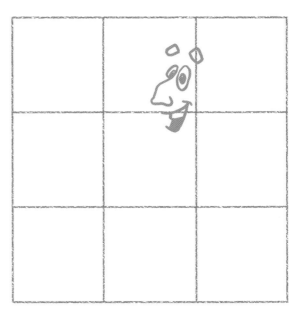

2.

Draw in the big beard and the puffy material under his chin.

Draw a curved line for his stomach, which flows onto his legs. Add the other leg and his feet. Draw in another curved line going from the puffy material to the back of his hip.

3.

Draw a curved line in front of his stomach for his robe. Add the arm and puffy robe cuff. Draw in the right hand.

Draw the other arm, cuff and hand. Draw in a backward "S" that goes from his ear to the recently drawn hand.

4.

Draw in the scepter and the crown. Add the spots on the robe. Draw a ring on the king's finger. Draw in the king's vest to finish this stage.

Artist Tip:

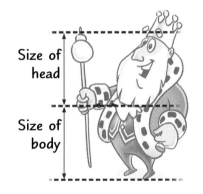

Size of head

Size of body

In cartooning, we can give our character personality by emphasizing their main features. This good-hearted king makes up in personality what he lacks in height. This personality is emphasized by using his most expressive feature, which is his face and head. Notice how the head is as big as the rest of the body combined. The henchman in this book has a small head because he is not very clever, but a big upper body to emphasise his strength. The henchman's strength is the dominant feature. See if you can design cartoon characters with emphasized attributes.

5.

Kings wore many different colored robes. Red, purple, blue, and yellow are considered to be royal colors.

Queen

A jolly king wouldn't be a jolly king without a jolly queen. This queen was made to accompany the drawing of the king in this book. See if you can draw them side by side.

1.

Begin by drawing a grid with two squares going across and four down.

Start by drawing in the eyes and nose. Move on to the cheeks and chin. Draw in the three-quarter circle for the earring. Draw in the collar that goes from the earring to just under the nose.

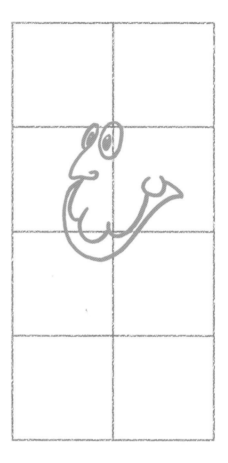

2.

Add a circle for the clasped hands.

Draw in the hair shape and the upper cheek. Add the arms around to the clasped hands. Add the sides of her dress and the pattern on it.

3.

Draw the crown on a slight angle. Add just a couple of eyelashes on each eye and some lines for her hair. Draw in her mouth and add the squiggly line for her fingers. Finish by drawing in the wavy line for the bottom of her dress.

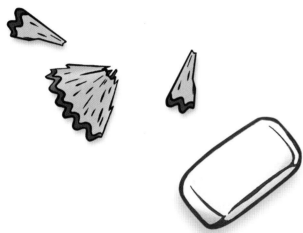

4.

Queens wear shiny crowns with bright jewels in them. Notice the white spots that highlight her crown. You can make these with correction pen or white dabs of paint.

Superhero

Superheroes are a villain's worst enemy. They arrive just in time to save the day, foil the villain's evil plan and rescue the innocent victim. Superheroes have special powers that ordinary people only dream of. Here we have a classic superhero speeding to the aid of a citizen in trouble.

1.

Begin by drawing a grid with four equal squares going across and three down.

Notice his head shape. Both the henchman in this book and this superhero have a thick neck, large chin, and small forehead, which makes them look tough. A large upper body with thick arms and small legs, which we are about to draw, adds to this effect.

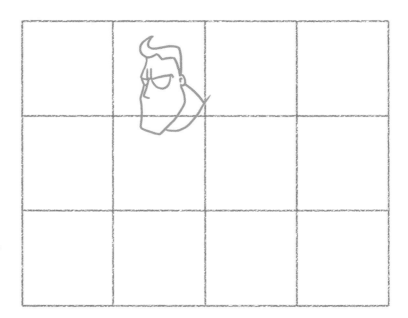

2.

Add the cape and the shape for his chest going in to his arm. Notice the hand is very simple. Draw in the mouth to finish this stage.

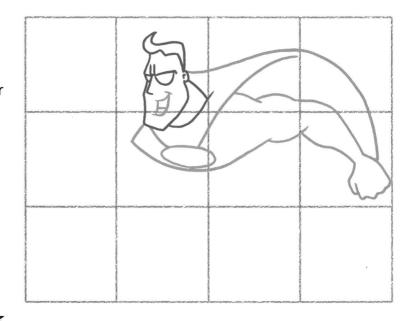

3.

Draw in his other muscly arm getting thinner as it reaches his wrist. Draw his torso getting smaller as it reaches his stomach. Add the bottom of the cape.

4.

Add his stomach muscle lines. As mentioned before, add the small legs. Study the clenched fist on his forward hand. Finish with his pupils in his eyes. We have left his emblem bare so you can make up your own symbol. You could even use the first letter of your name.

5.

Superheroes often have bright and contrasting colors and are seen in action poses. Do you think you could recreate this superhero in different poses?

Published in 2015 by **Windmill Books**,
an Imprint of Rosen Publishing,
29 East 21st Street, New York, NY 10010.

Copyright © 2015 by Hinkler Books

Written and illustrated by Damien Toll.
With thanks to Jared Gow.

Library of Congress Cataloging-in-Publication Data
Toll, Damien.
 Drawing awesome cartoon characters / Damien Toll.
     pages cm. — (Drawing is awesome!)
 Includes index.
ISBN 978-1-4777-5459-7 (pbk.)
ISBN 978-1-4777-5476-4 (6 pack)
ISBN 978-1-4777-5472-6 (library binding)
1. Cartoon characters—Juvenile literature.
2. Drawing—Technique—Juvenile literature.
 I. Title.
NC1764.T65 2015
741.5'1—dc23
                                    2014027093

Manufactured in the United States of America
CPSIA Compliance Information: Batch # CW15WM: For Further Information contact
Rosen Publishing, New York, New York at 1-800-237-9932